THE DIAMOND OF SUCCESS

THE P'S TO WINNING

JEFF RAMEY

CONTENTS

Acknowledgements V
Forward vii
Prologue X

Chapter 1   Potential 1
Chapter 2   Purpose 6
Chapter 3   Passion 10
Chapter 4   Positive Mindset 14
Chapter 5   Perspiration Equity 17
Chapter 6   Personal Sacrifice 22
Chapter 7   Powerful Leadership 25
Chapter 8   Positive Periphery 29
Chapter 9   Precise Persistent Focus 34
Chapter 10   Purposeful Planning & Preparation 37
Chapter 11   Poise 40
Chapter 12   Pridelessness 43
Chapter 13   Professionalism 47
Chapter 14   Progressive Thinking 50
Chapter 15   Pursuit of Excellence 54
Chapter 16   Perseverance 57
Chapter 17   Perspective 60

Conclusion 64
Appendix A: "Big 33" 33 Life Lessons Learned
                    on the Diamond 68
Appendix B: The P's To Winning 85
Appendix C: The Diamond of Success 89
Credits 90

Jeff and I played together at Indiana University and I vividly remember a very passionate, humble, loyal, and hardworking teammate. He demonstrated remarkable leadership skills at an early age and he has taken those special characteristics from his experiences in amateur and professional baseball and assembled a masterpiece for all chosen professions. One person with passion is greater than 10,000 without and this book will help you become that one person and bring you closer to that leader you want to be for your team.

~Billy Gernon-Head Baseball Coach
Western Michigan University

ACKNOWLEDGEMENTS

First of all, I'd like to thank God for blessing me with the talent to play the game of baseball. I worked hard but without the God given abilities to begin with none of my successes would have been possible.

To my Dad-thank you for your unconditional love, unwavering faith, and perfect example of what a father should be. The only difference between my success and the failures of others was the fact that I had you as my father.

To my wife, Lara, and my daughters, Olivia and Katie-I love you with all my heart. Thank you for showing me what life is truly about.

To my best friend Pat Rigsby- thank you for your loyalty. You are more than my best friend. You are my brother.

To my college roommates- Joe Sturtz and Dave Snedden- I'm not sure why God placed the three of us together in Bloomington, Indiana but, I am forever thankful. I couldn't imagine my life without you guys in it.

To my workout partner and roomie, Mike Smith, thank you for giving me a front row seat to the finest season in college baseball history. More importantly, thank you for taking me under your wing and showing me what it means to be a true professional.

To all my former coaches- Darrell Donnally, Bruce Johnson, R.D. Baker, Ron Crabtree, Jon Daniels, John Tipton, Stan Doddridge, Dave Napierkowski, Ken Wheeler, Sam McGraw, Bob Morgan, Steve Parrill, Kevin Howard, Dean Schuler, Dennis Hegarty, Dan Kubacki, Donnie Scott, Mark Berry, and the late Lowell Fenton, Bill Newman, Bob Welch, John Ison, Tommy Dunbar, and Jim Hickman-thank you for sharing your knowledge of the game. The time and energy you invested in me will never be forgotten.

To my former teammates- thank you for the memories and more importantly the friendships. I couldn't imagine playing with a better group of guys.

To the late Gene Bennett- thank you for giving me the opportunity to be a professional baseball player. To get drafted by a Hall-of – Fame scout is truly humbling.

To Tim Saunders- thank you for recommending me for a scholarship to Indiana University. Because of you I got to spend three years at one of the nation's finest universities with some of the finest people one could ever meet.

Lastly, to all my former players- as a coach I strived to be a blessing to you but in reality you were a blessing to me.

FORWARD

I am honored that Jeff asked me to write the forward to his new book, <u>The Diamond of Success: The P's to Winning.</u> The book is a wonderful compilation and playbook to success in baseball, sports, and life. You will find the book easy to read and packed full of instruction. Jeff is a lifelong friend and my former roommate at Indiana University. We played college baseball together for three glorious years. I've been blessed over the last 25 years to see Jeff grow as a baseball player, professional, and person.

It doesn't surprise me that Jeff wants to give back and impact lives. Jeff's book is inspirational, fact-based, and full of wisdom that will help all that read it. I experienced great joy and pride as I read each page. The stories are real, time-tested, and applicable for today. Jeff is by far the most inquisitive person that I've met in my sports and professional career. He lives for knowledge and is on a quest to unlock the "secret sauce" to success. His passion to answer deep life questions of successful people is well-documented in the following pages.

As for me, I grew up in Piqua, Ohio, a small blue collar town north of Dayton. My parents were high school sweethearts and married at 18. Neither went to college. They worked hard and did their best to provide for a family of four children. I'm the third child and the first to go to college. We struggled as a family financially, which I didn't realize until I left for college. Attending IU as a student-athlete was my life, escape, and roadmap to what was possible on and off the field. Reading *The Diamond of Success: The P's to Winning* led me to reflect on my life and my time with Jeff. As I worked through each page and chapter, it became clear that my path to success in all facets of my life are contained in the book. Every chapter is honest, rich in experience and rooted by Jeff digging deeper to better understand what drives success. If you are looking to unlock your potential, you will find it in Jeff's book.

I'm so proud of Jeff for sharing his life lessons, experiences, and findings from asking the tough questions of successful people. The book is applicable to athletes at all levels of baseball, or any sport for that matter. While anchored in athletics, his work will impact business professionals or anyone that is looking to maximize their potential. It is a must read for athletes, teams, business professionals and, most importantly, our youth.

I genuinely believe that God granted each one of us with unlimited potential. Many aspire, but few obtain. Jeff has provided a "playbook" to guide you on the path to realizing your potential. Read carefully, study, reflect, and take action on every chapter. Knowing Jeff, nothing will bring him more joy.

-Mike " Smitty" Smith

Entrepreneur, former Senior Vice President Williamson- Dickie's Manufacturing Co. (retired), former Professional Baseball Player and Director of Player Development with the Texas Rangers,

Former 1st Team All-American, National Player of the Year, and 2-time Big Ten Player of the Year at Indiana University, only Triple Crown winner in the history of NCAA Division 1 Baseball (.490 BA, 27 HR, 95 RBIs)

PROLOGUE

I once knew a boy who seemed destined to play the game of baseball. If there was ever a person that had a hand dealt in his favor it was him. He was born in a town that had produced multiple major league all-stars and World Series champions. He was raised in a neighborhood of kids that, though much older, not only loved baseball but took him under their wing and showed him how to play the game. The local union hall only a few feet from his front doorstep provided the perfect brick wall to throw a ball against anytime he so chose. While his neighbor's large backyard provided the ultimate wiffle ball field to hold sandlot games that would sometimes last from dawn to dusk. All this combined with a father that was always there for practice, support, and encouragement, made a successful baseball career seem like a forgone conclusion.

Early on as he transitioned from the sandlots to organized little league, it was quickly evident that he had also been blessed with the necessary skills to be successful. All- star teams, championships, and baseball camp most valuable player awards soon became the norm. One coach even commented on his baseball camp evaluation, "If you continue to work hard and never become satisfied you could be a pro someday!" While some kids would have become complacent or succumb to the pressure of such lofty expectations, he embraced the challenge and only worked harder. Baseball became his passion.

As he transitioned from little league to senior league, his desire and work ethic were extraordinary but the skill set that once stood out was being sabotaged by his physical limitations. While puberty was providing his peers with growth spurts and newfound muscular physiques, he was stuck in the body of a prepubescent little leaguer. The once powerful bat was diminished to fly balls rarely reaching the outfield grass and the fastball that once made hitters tremble was now seen as nothing more than batting practice. If this wasn't embarrassing enough, he was not selected to the all-star team for the first time. As you can imagine tears of sadness were shed and thoughts of quitting crept into his head.

If not for the wisdom and love of his father, this could have been the end of what once seemed like a promising baseball career. "Trust me, you are gonna grow and when you do you are gonna be better than all these guys" his father told him. Despite his skepticism, he decided to put his trust and faith in those words. He made a list of everyone on that all-star team and placed it on his dresser so he could see it on a daily basis. He went back to work more determined than ever. He wasn't gonna be satisfied until he was better than each and every name on the list.

As he entered high school, with several names crossed off the list, his physical limitations once again hindered his progress. As a 5'2" 105 pound freshman, he still battled his physical deficiencies. However, he continued to trust the process and embrace the daily grind of getting better. While he dressed varsity as a freshman, failure and embarrassment quickly struck again when he was left off the post season roster come tournament time. Once again tears of sadness and thoughts of quitting crept into his head but once again the wisdom and love of his father intervened. "Trust me, you have them right where you want them. Fundamentally you are better than them. You have a stronger work ethic and desire than them. You are gonna get stronger and when you do you will be better than them all." He once again put his trust and faith in those words and went back to work even more determined than the last time.

He sought out a track coach to help with his running speed. He threw weighted baseballs to improve his arm strength. He lifted weights to get stronger. He snuck into the high schools batting cage multiple nights each week to work on his hitting. Then as he began to grow, just as his father predicted, the power in his bat and the zip on his fastball returned, while his desire, determination, and work ethic had never left. The individual accolades, team championships, and most valuable player awards soon followed. Eventually he had marked every name off the list and just prior to his senior season he received a division one baseball scholarship to a school in the prestigious Big Ten Conference.

CHAPTER 1

POTENTIAL

Potential is the latent qualities or abilities that <u>may</u> be developed and lead to future success.

"Potential means you haven't done anything yet."
(Bill Parcells)

Billy Beane was a 6'4" first round selection of the New York Mets in the 1980 Major League Baseball Draft. If not for the threat of him attending Stanford University to play both football and baseball, he would have been the first overall selection in the entire draft. In other words, most experts felt he had more <u>potential</u> than any player in the entire country. However, due the question of his sign-ability he lasted until the 23rd overall pick. None the less, a player of Beane's size, power, and speed was considered a can't miss major league prospect.

Lenny Dykstra on the other hand, was a 5'10" 13th round selection of the Mets in the 1981 Major League Baseball Draft. Despite having outstanding speed, he was considered a marginal prospect at best. There wasn't a scout in the country who felt Dykstra had more potential than Beane. However, despite his inferior physical talent, Lenny Dykstra would go on to have the far better career of the two.

In the book Moneyball, they explain why it was Dykstra and not Beane that was able to maximize his potential as a baseball player:

> *Physically, Lenny didn't belong in the same league with Billy. He was half Billy's size and had a fraction of Billy's promise-which is why the Met's didn't draft him until the 13th round. Mentally, Lenny was superior. During a spring training game, Billy remembers sitting with Lenny in the dugout while watching the opposing pitcher warm up. Lenny says, "Who's the big dumb-ass out there on the hill?" And I say, "Lenny, you are kidding me right? That's Steve Carlton. He's maybe the greatest left-hander in the history of the game." Lenny says, "Oh yeah, so what's he got?" And I say, "Lenny, come on. Steve Carlton. He's got heat and maybe the nastiest slider in the history of the game." Lenny sits there for a minute as if he's taking it all in. Finally, he says, "Shit, I'll stickhim!" I'm sitting there thinking, that's a magazine cover out there on the mound and all Lenny can think is "shit I'll stick him."*

"There is no heavier burden than an unfulfilled potential."
(Charles Schulz)

Application:

"You have the potential to be a pro someday if you continue to work hard and never become satisfied!" As a 12 year old, those were the words written on my camper evaluation sheet after winning the camp Most Valuable Player Award.

As a 14 year old I was not selected for the league all-star team after the coaches decided that I did not have the potential of some of the other players my age.

As a high school freshman I was left off our high school teams post season roster because our coach felt I did not have the potential to help us compete for a state championship.

As a high school senior I received a scholarship from Indiana University because Coach Bob Morgan felt I had the potential to be a solid Division 1 baseball player.

As a junior in college I was drafted by the Cincinnati Reds because Scout Gene Bennett felt I had the potential to become a future major leaguer.

As a rookie playing in Billings, Montana my manager, former big league catcher Donnie Scott, called me into his office to tell me that he felt I had the potential to catch in the Big Leagues.

The point I'm trying to illustrate is that potential is important. It is in large part what determines whether we do or do not get opportunities. The hope and future success of teams and organizations is in large part predicated on potential. However, as the example of Billy Beane and Lenny Dykstra illustrates, great potential is by no means an accurate predictor of future success.

A players potential is in large part based upon three factors: size, power, and speed. These are all things that can be seen with the naked eye or measured with a tape measure, radar gun, or stop-watch. However, there are things like heart, desire, and mindset that cannot be measured. These are referred to as intangibles and these are the qualities that often determine the success of a baseball player.

Year after year, scouts and recruiters scour the country measuring a player's size, power, and speed while trying to get a feel for their heart, desire, and mindset. Thousands of miles are traveled and hundreds of games are watched, all in an effort to predict a player's potential for future success; searching for that next hot shot recruit or major league prospect. Those thought to have the most potential receive the larger scholarships and signing bonuses, while those with the least potential are left to fight for whatever is left over. That's if they even get an opportunity at all.

However, as illustrated above, potential does not guarantee success. Success can only be obtained if that potential is developed. As the late Angie Garrido put it, at some point a prospect has to become a player.

Potential is what you can become but make sure it's not all you become.

They said it...

"I hate the word potential. Potential means you haven't gotten it done."
(Alex Rodriquez)

THERE IS NOTHING WORSE THAN WASTED TALENT

CHAPTER 2

PURPOSE

Purpose is a person's intentions, objectives, and sense of resolve or determination.

"The secret to success is consistency of purpose."
(Benjamin Disraell)

We have all heard of Alex Rodriquez, Bryce Harper, and Mike Trout, guys who only needed a "cup of coffee" in the minor leagues before becoming major league superstars.

Most have heard of Dave Winfield, Bob Horner, Pete Incaviglia, John Olerud, Jim Abbott, and most recently Mike Leake, guys who went straight from their perspective colleges to the major leagues without spending a day in the minors.

But how about guys like Brian Esposito, Christ Coste, J.C. Boscan, Max St. Pierre, and John Lindsey?

These are guys who toiled in the minor leagues for more than a decade before reaching the major leagues.

- Brian Esposito played 11 seasons for six different organizations before reaching the major leagues.
- Chris Coste went undrafted despite being a three time All-American at Division III Concordia College. He eventually signed with an independent league and spent 12 seasons bouncing between the independent and minor leagues. It wasn't until 2006 at the age of 33 years old that he could call himself a major leaguer.
- J.C. Boscan signed a professional contract as a 16 year old kid out of Venezuela. It would be 14 years later before he reached the major leagues for the first time.
- Max St. Pierre signed as a 17 year old and like Boscan, spent 14 seasons in the minor leagues before reaching "The Show".
- But none of the above topped John Lindsey, who after 16 seasons and 1,571 games in the minor leagues, finally realized his dream of playing in the major leagues.

Why would these guys be willing to spend so many years playing baseball for minimal pay under less than optimal living conditions?

Why were they willing to persevere when most would have given up?

Why were they able to overcome so many obstacles when most would have thought they were too difficult to overcome?

The answer is in their "why".

They had such a deep seeded passion and love for the game that it would not allow them to quit.

They were going to simply keep playing until someone literally ripped the uniform off of them.

They weren't playing for fame, fortune, or to please others. Instead, they were playing for a genuine love of the game.

That's the only thing that allowed them to persevere and overcome so many obstacles to get there.

"When every action has a purpose, every action has a result."
(Greg Pitts)

Application:

Your purpose is your "why".

Your "why" will drive your actions and behaviors. It will serve as your motivation and inspiration during times of adversity. When you don't feel like practicing, you'll do it anyway. When you make a mistake, you'll find a way to fix it. When others lose their desire and determination, yours will persevere.

Winning players love the game of baseball. It's why they play. They have specific, clearly defined goals with a never ending desire and commitment to what it is they want to achieve.

Winning teams are created when each member of the team not only knows their purpose but accepts their purpose. An under-standing of purpose and acceptance of purpose are vital to both individual and team success.

The more members of a team that play because they love the game and understand and accept their purpose for being there, the more successful the individual player will be and the team will be.

Why do you play the game?

We all have different reasons for why we play the game of baseball. Many play for the opportunity at fortune and fame. Some play to please a parent or impress a girlfriend. Others play just because it's something to do with their friends. But what happens when a parent passes away, your girlfriend breaks up with you, or your friends no longer want to play? Will you still have the desire and determination to continue on? The answer is most likely not.

The only sustainable "why" is a genuine love for the game.

They said it...

> **"Find something you love and go after it with all your heart." (Jim Abbott)**

WHY YOU DO WHAT YOU DO

CHAPTER 3

PASSION

Passion is an intense desire or enthusiasm for something.

"Nothing great was ever achieved without enthusiasm."
(Ralph Waldo Emerson)

In the spring of 1963, 22-year old Peter Edward Rose, showed up for Spring Training ready to prove that he belonged in the big leagues. After hitting over .300 in the two previous minor league seasons, it was known that the kid could hit but, what wasn't known was the impact he'd have on the game with his hustle.

During one particular spring training game, while playing the Yankees, Mickey Mantle hit a towering home run over the left field fence. Most left fielders would have simply stood pat and watched the ball fly over the fence but, Pete Rose wasn't like most left fielders. Instead he sprinted to the wall and attempted to catch the ball even though the ball was long gone. Once Mantle rounded the bases and returned to the dugout, Whitey Ford said to Mantle, "Did you see Charlie Hustle out there?"(Hence, the birth of "Charlie Hustle")

Even though Whitey Ford was essentially making fun of Rose's futile attempt at robbing Mantle's homer, he made the team following that spring training in 1963 and would go on to win the Rookie of the Year Award. Twenty three seasons later, he had hustled his way into the record books and hearts of baseball fans across America.

He would go on to become one of the game's all-time greats, finishing his career as a three time World Champion and the games career hit leader. He would have been a sure fire first ballot Hall-of-Famer if not for his on-field and off the field transgressions.

However, what many of us will remember about Peter Edward Rose is not the championships and the hits but, the hustle and passion for which he played the game.

The sprint to first base after a walk, the airborne head first dive into third, and the way he'd spike the ball off the turf after the third out of an inning will forever be etched in our mind.

Pete Rose was talented but, far from the most talented.

However, I do believe that he was one of the most passionate, if not THE most passionate player to ever play the game. He was so passionate that Sparky Anderson once said:

> *"Pete Rose would run through hell in a gasoline suit to play the game of baseball!"*

"Passion is when you put more energy into something than is required to do it. It is more than just enthusiasm and excitement. Passion is

ambition that is materialized into action to put as much heart, mind, body, and soul into something as is humanly possible." (Unknown)

Application:

Potential matters. A clear sense of purpose matters. But potential and a clear sense of purpose are useless without passion.

You can have great potential. You can have a genuine love for the game. But without a true passion for the game, you will not take the massive action necessary to achieve <u>sustained</u> success.

In fact, passion is so important and powerful, that many less talented players have had more success than those more talented, simply because they practice, prepare, and play the game with more passion and enthusiasm.

And not only are they more successful individually but, the contagiousness of their enthusiasm elevates the performance of their teammates and their team as a whole.

I'm not recommending you "run through hell in a gasoline suit" to play the game of baseball but I am recommending that you "play like your hair is on fire".

Play the game with passion, enthusiasm, and energy.

You cannot maximize your talent as a player or team without it.

They said it...

"Do what you love to do and give it your very best. Whether it's business or baseball, or the theater, or any field. If you don't love what you're doing and you can't give it your best, get out of it. Life is too short. You'll be an old man before you know it."(Al Lopez)

ENTHUSIASM IS CONTAGIOUS

CHAPTER 4

POSITIVE MINDSET

Positive mindset is an established set of values or beliefs marked by optimism.

"Make sure your worst enemy doesn't live between your ears."
(Laird Hamilton)

I have seen time and time again the power of a positive mindset. One example of this was in 1992, shortly after I'd been drafted by the Cincinnati Reds. Following a brief two week mini spring training in Billings, Montana, we loaded the bus for our first professional games against the Dodgers in Great Falls, Montana. Our nervous energy and butterfly filled bellies made any chance of sleeping an impossibility. The four hour bus ride was filled with conversation, movies, card games, and plenty of friendly banter and tomfoolery. At some point, the question arose, "What are you going to do if you don't make it to the major leagues?" A large majority of us answered the question, me included. At the time, I didn't think much of it but, as time has gone on I think about two things. First of all, who initiated the question? I can't remember the name of the player who started the conversation but, what I do remember is that he didn't make it to the major leagues. Secondly,

I think about the three players who I specifically remember not answering the question. Chad Mottola. Tim Belk. Eric Owens. All three of them went on to play in the big leagues. I now know why they sat there in silence. I truly believe that <u>they weren't going to let any negative thoughts creep into their minds. Their mindset was that they had been successful and they were going to continue being successful all the way to "The Show".</u>

> *"Ability is what you are capable of doing.*
> *Motivation determines what you do. Attitude*
> *determines how well you do it."*
> *(Lou Holtz)*

Application:

There are only three things you can control as an athlete: your preparation, your effort, and your attitude. We will discuss preparation and effort in later chapters but, many athletes have the attitude that success is beyond their reach. Sometimes this is due to the fear and insecurities created by past failures. Sometimes it is due to perceived physical limitations. Other times it's due to listening to the naysayers and critics and allowing their insecurities and inadequacies to become their own.

However, winners recognize that they have power over their attitude and they choose to be positive. As Henry Ford once said, "whether you think you can or think you can't you are right." It's your choice. Winners think positive with affirmative thoughts and self-talk. They don't dwell on past failures but instead learn from them and draw strength on their past successes.

Your mindset will often be your most formidable opponent. Negative self-talk and self- doubt will create self-imposed limitations and fictitious obstacles that only impede your path to success. Therefore, the first step to success is believing that your goals can be accomplished. Then once your mindset is right it will set your body in motion to find a way to make your goals a reality.

Don't sell yourself short. Don't listen to that inner voice telling you that you can't. Don't listen to the critics and naysayers. Realize that the naysayers are often unsuccessful people who love nothing more than to destroy your plans for success. Don't create self-imposed limitations and fictitious obstacles. Think success not failure. By thinking success you will plan for success, prepare for success, and achieve success.

They said it...

> "The more you play baseball the less it depends on your athletic ability. It's a mental war more than anything."(Alex Rodriquez)

WIN THE BATTLEFIELD OF THE MIND

CHAPTER 5

PERSPIRATION EQUITY

Perspiration equity is an increased value in something earned from labor or hard work.

"No one ever drowned in sweat."
(Lou Holtz)

When the Philadelphia Phillies signed Roy Halladay in the winter of 2010, they knew they were getting a dominant ace. With six all-star appearances and a Cy Young Award already on his resume, he was widely regarded as the best pitcher in the game.

The manager of the Phillies, Charlie Manual, was fully aware of the caliber of pitcher they'd acquired but what he didn't realize was that he was getting one of the hardest workers in all of baseball.

On the first day of spring training, Charlie Manual arrived at his office at 530AM. Typically this would be a time of solitude where he could gather his thoughts and plan for the day without any interruptions.

However, after noticing a light on in the workout room, he walked back to turn it off. He assumed that someone had left it on from the day before. However, as he got closer he heard music. Once he got to the room, he realized that he wasn't alone. The newly acquired Roy Halladay was drenched in sweat, already a full hour into his morning workout.

Maybe this was an isolated incident. Maybe he couldn't sleep due the excitement of joining a new team and decided to go ahead and come in early. Maybe he had some obligations later in the day and this was the only time he could get in his workout.

But what everyone would soon find out was that this was just Roy Halladay being Roy Halladay. He was the hardest worker in the room not just some of the time but all the time.

> *"I can still remember the first day we met. It was 5:45 a.m. on the first day of spring training when I arrived. He was finishing his breakfast but his clothes were soaking wet. I asked if it was raining when he got in. He laughed and said, 'No, I just finished my workout.' I knew right then—he was the real deal."*
> *(Chase Utley)*

It didn't matter what time of year it was…

> *"Roy Halladay walked into the visitors' clubhouse at Camden Yards drenched in sweat, wearing an expression of exhaustion in the hours before a September game in Baltimore. The Blue Jays' ace looked like he had just finished flipping oversized*

tires in the stadium parking lot amidst Maryland's fatiguing humidity. This was not all that unusual of a scene -- Halladay's workout routine during his playing days bordered on legendary -- except for one important bit of detail. This was the final day of the 2008 regular season, and the pitcher had no more starts left on the schedule. His next outing would be Opening Day, seven months in the future."

Or who was or wasn't watching…

"I never knew Roy personally but his work ethic impacted me from the one time we squared off in a spring training game in Lakeland. We each threw a few innings and I had gone to the clubhouse, ate lunch, and showered up. I was walking out to my car and saw Roy drenched in sweat running poles on the back fields. I've never forgotten that day as it was clear he never needed the cameras or coaches around to push himself and no matter what he was going to get his work done. That's the Roy Halladay I will always remember." (Max Scherzer)

"Patience, persistence, and perspiration make an unbeatable combination of success." (Napoleon Hill)

Application:

We are often led to believe that unless we are born with a certain level of natural talent we cannot achieve success. While there is no denying the advantages of natural talent, without hard work it will be wasted. In fact it has been said that "hard work beats talent when talent doesn't work hard".

Winners are not always the most talented but, they are often the most committed. They take great pride in doing the work others are not willing to do. They don't just do what is required; they do more than is required. They realize that there is a high correlation between the work put in and the results going out.

There is no way to avoid it. The process of success is a mental and physical grind. While everyone wants success, very few are willing to commit to the process. Winners are not only committed to the process, they embrace it. They don't procrastinate or make excuses. Instead they attack their goals with a persistent work ethic that makes anything other than success highly unlikely.

They simply care like no one else, prepare like no one else, and therefore excel like no one else.

They said it...

"In order to excel you must be completely dedicated. You must also be prepared to work hard and be willing to accept constructive criticism. Without 100% dedication, you won't be able to do this."(Willie Mays)

"There may be people with more talent than you but there is no excuse for anyone to work harder than you do."(Derek Jeter)

GET COMFORTABLE, BEING UNCOMFORTABLE

CHAPTER 6

PERSONAL SACRIFICE

Personal sacrifice is giving up something you want or something you desire in order to help others or advance a cause.

"No man achieves great success who is unwilling to make personal sacrifice."
(Napoleon Hill)

In 1966, Dennis Hegarty was a walk on at Miami-Dade Community College. Legendary Miami-Dade baseball coach Demie Mainieri described Hegarty as "showing no natural tools to play college baseball." He even tried to get Hegarty to quit the team as he saw no possible way that he would ever see the field. However, an injury to the starting left fielder during the Florida State Junior College Tournament, forced Hegarty to play. He not only played but played well, even hitting a game winning home run off future major leaguer Gary Gentry in the Junior College World Series. In 1967, the player Hegarty replaced, Preston Pratt, was healthy and ready to reclaim his starting position. However, despite his superior talent, his reluctance to follow the rules forced Coach Mainieri to remove him from the team. The next morning, following Pratt's dismissal, several players including Dennis Hegarty showed up in Coach Mainieri's office. The players pleaded for him to reinstate Pratt to the team. They felt that not only could Pratt help them win but by keeping him on the team it could also help Pratt mature. <u>When Coach Mainieri asked Hegarty if he realized that reinstating Pratt to the team would cost him his starting spot, he said yes but, thought it was for the betterment of the team and Pratt</u>. Pratt was reinstated but never truly lived up to his potential as a baseball player. Dennis Hegarty, on the other hand, would go on to play at Ohio University alongside future Hall-of-Famer Mike Schmidt, leading them to the 1970 College World Series. Following his playing career, he became a Hall-of Fame high school baseball coach in my hometown of Portsmouth, Ohio.

> *"If you don't sacrifice for what you want,*
> *what you want becomes the sacrifice."*
> *(Unknown)*

Application:

Winning requires tremendous sacrifice both personally and as a unit. Personally you must be willing to sacrifice time away from your family, friends, and social activities. As a team, each member must be willing to sacrifice personal accomplishments for team accomplishments if that is what's best for team success.

The ability to balance individual goals with team goals is challenging but necessary. Winning teams find a way to work together with a common vision, clear sense of purpose, and an unbreakable commitment to each other. This can only be accomplished with great sacrifice, both personally and collectively.

They Said it...

"When you are a part of a team, you stand up for your teammates. Your loyalty is to them. You protect them through good and bad, because they'd do the same for you." (Yogi Berra)

T.E.A.M. = <u>T</u>ogether <u>E</u>veryone <u>A</u>chieves <u>M</u>ore

---

SACRIFICE THE ME FOR THE WE

CHAPTER 7

POWERFUL LEADERSHIP

Powerful leadership is the act of leading with great power, prestige, and influence.

> *"A leader is someone who knows the way,*
> *goes the way, and shows the way."*
> **(John Maxwell)**

Unless you've shopped for a car in Huntington, West Virginia you've probably never heard the name Lance Daniels. However, of all my former teammates none exemplified powerful leadership more than him. This was never more evident than prior to the opening game of our senior year. After leaving the bitter cold of Ohio behind, we traveled to Florida to open our season against Vero Beach High School. With no outdoor practices or games under our belt, we knew that facing a top ten team from Florida, with an impressive 16-4 record, would be a tough task. Following our pre game batting practice, our head coach, John Tipton, gathered us down the left field line for some words of encouragement...so we thought. Instead, he essentially told us to do our best but, the fact that they'd already played twenty games was going to be too much of an obstacle to overcome. Even though I was stunned by his lack of faith, I followed the pack as we began to jog back to the dugout. However, there was one player that never moved from the left field line. As we approached the dugout, we heard Lance Daniels instruct us all to "get back here". As we turned and jogged back, he gathered us in a circle just as Coach Tipton had done moments earlier. However, he delivered a much different message. He basically told us to forget what we'd just heard and to go out there and "kick their A**!" And that is exactly what we did. I have to believe that if Lance Daniels would have joined the pack and jogged back to the dugout following our coaches' pre-game speech; we would not have won that game. But because he didn't, we not only pulled off the upset but, went on to have a very successful season. Lance Daniel's powerful leadership had a lot to do with that.

> *"If your actions inspire others to dream more, learn more, do more, and become more, you are a leader."*
> **(John Quincy Adams)**

Application:

There is no denying the influence of leadership on winning and losing. I have played on talented teams that underachieved due to poor leadership just as I have played on less talented teams that overachieved due to strong leadership.

Powerful leadership is not only critical for success but, it is often THE difference maker.

While I have been fortunate to play with and for many powerful leaders, they each had their own leadership style. Some were more vocal while others led with their actions more than their words. However, the following commonalities are what made them all powerful leaders:

Loyalty- they were faithful and devoted to the team
Educated- they were knowledgeable about their craft
Accountable- they didn't make excuses or blame others
Dependable- they were trustworthy and reliable
Empowering- they motivated you to be your best and achieve more
Empathetic- they strived to respect and understand the feelings of others
Respected- they were highly regarded more for their professionalism than their talent
Sincere- they had a genuine love for the game and the people they played it with
Humble- they had a modest view of their own importance
Innovative- they were perpetual learners who were open to more effective ways
Passionate- they played and practiced with enthusiasm
People Focused-they had a genuine desire to serve others and establish meaningful relationships

They said it...

"I always cared more about winning more than anything else. That meant playing harder than anyone but that also meant trying to be a great teammate who made everyone around him better. That to me was what it was all about. It wasn't selfish or selfless, it was who I was at the core. I cared about everyone of my teammates and always tried to think of what might help them and what might get them going. If my style rubbed off on them, nothing made me happier." (Pete Rose)

LEAD, FOLLOW, OR GET OUT OF THE WAY

CHAPTER 8

POSITIVE PERIPHERY

Positive periphery is the perimeter of a circle that has a good, affirmative, or constructive quality or attribute

> *"Surround yourself with the dreamers and the doers, the believers and the thinkers, but most of all, surround yourself with those who see the greatness within you, even when you don't see it yourself." (Edmund Lee)*

In the summer of 2000, myself and Pat Rigsby, my former teammate and best friend, made the two hour trip from our hometown of Portsmouth, Ohio to Charleston, West Virginia. We went there to not only see our former player Dan Grummit play for the Charleston (SC) Riverdogs, the class A affiliate of the Tampa Bay Devil Rays, but to also catch a glimpse of his teammate Josh Hamilton, the number one ranked prospect in all of baseball.

Hamilton was the first overall pick in the 1999 Major League Baseball draft, receiving a signing bonus of $3.9 million dollars. This afforded his parents the opportunity to retire from their jobs, buy an RV, and travel with their son on his journey throughout the minor leagues.

Hamilton was regarded by many scouts and baseball experts to be one of the best prospects in the history of the game. After watching him play in person, I too thought I had just watched a soon-to-be major league star and future Hall of Famer. He had all the tools and at 6'4" 220 pounds he looked as if he'd been designed in a lab for the sole purpose of playing the game of baseball. And if that wasn't enough, after meeting him after the game, I left feeling as if he was one of the most humble and gracious people I'd ever met.

After his first two professional seasons he was living up to all the lofty expectations, hitting over .300 with double digit home runs, while displaying the speed and arm strength that would make him a future major league gold glover. He was on the fast track to the major leagues.

However, in the spring of 2001, while driving with his parents in Tampa, Florida, a dump truck ran a red light and slammed into the side of their vehicle. The impact of the collision left his mother and father with injuries requiring them to head back to their home-town of Raleigh, North Carolina for surgery and months of rehab for their injuries. Hamilton was the least injured during the collision, suffering only a "minor" back injury. However, the months following the accident would turn out to be a major turning point not only in his professional baseball career but his life.

After being placed on the disabled list to rehab from his injuries, Hamilton had more free time on his hands than ever before. This in conjunction with being away from his parents for the first time, gave him a new found freedom and plenty of idol time.

Josh's parents warned him years prior, "If people are doing things they shouldn't be doing at a place they shouldn't be, if you hang out there long enough, you'll start doing them too." Despite his parent's words of wisdom, he began to spend hours upon hours at a local tattoo parlor. His mornings were spent at the Devil Rays spring training facility doing rehab on his back while his afternoons and evenings were spent hanging out at the tattoo parlor.

Within weeks his tattoo collection went from zero to nearly twenty but, even though his parents and those around him were perplexed by his new found body art, the tattoos were the least of his worries.

One day after hanging out at the tattoo parlor all evening, the tattoo artists asked if he'd like to go out with them after they closed the shop. Even though he'd never been to a bar or drank a sip of alcohol in his life, he said yes.

After drinking his first beer at a local bar, Josh and his new found "friends" headed to the local strip club before heading to the home of one of the tattoo artists. It was there that he completed the trifecta by having his first drink of alcohol, visiting his first strip club, and doing his first line of cocaine all in the same night. This wasn't exactly the Triple Crown he'd dreamed of.

Little did he know at the time but, the kid who did not attend his high school prom due to his fear of being around people who would put him in a compromising position and possibly jeopardize his career, was beginning down a path of destruction that would not only cast a huge shadow of doubt over his once promising baseball career but put him on the brink of death.

The next several years were filled with stints in and out of drug rehabilitation and multiple suspensions by Major League Baseball for violating the league's substance abuse policy. The vision and dream of a successful baseball career was quickly being replaced by a sheer desire to survive and overcome his addiction to drugs and alcohol.

Eventually, through faith and surrounding himself with the right people, Josh Hamilton would overcome his addictions, reach the major leagues, and even win a Most Valuable Player Award in 2010. By most people's standards, despite missing out on the prime years of his career, Josh Hamilton was a very successful major league baseball player. He played a total of nine seasons finishing with a career batting average of .290 with 200 career home runs. He won a batting title in 2010. He was a five-time all-star, three-time Silver Slugger Award winner, played in a World Series, and put on a show in the 2008 Home Run Derby that will be talked about forever.

However, I have to believe that Josh Hamilton has to wonder at times how his career and his life would have been different if he'd never ventured into that tattoo parlor and just said "NO" when he was asked to go out with his newfound "friends".

"You are the average of the five people
you spend the most time with."
(Jim Rohm)

Application:

It cannot be denied that our environment shapes our habits, attitudes, and mindset. Therefore, it is important to surround yourself with people who are positive, uplifting, and empowering. Don't let negative influencers pollute your environment. Do whatever is necessary to avoid the negative naysayers for they will do nothing but sabotage your plan for success.

They said it...

"There was a guy who hung around the team, especially around Howe. He wore his hair in a Mohawk. Nobody knew for sure what he did or his real name. They called him Rooster. But he supplied cocaine to Steve. Rooster would show up and then Steve would disappear for three days."

Ken Reitz, former major Leaguer on former teammate Steve Howe, the former Major League All-Star and World Series Champion who was suspended seven times by Major League Baseball due to his drug and alcohol addictions

CHOOSE YOUR FRIENDS WISELY

CHAPTER 9

PRECISE PERSISTENT FOCUS

Precise, persistent focus is a concentration level that is marked by consistency, exactness, accuracy, and careful attention to detail.

> *"The successful warrior is an average*
> *man with a laser like focus."*
> **(Bruce Lee)**

In 1992, Mike Smith, a former college teammate of mine, was named Big Ten Player of the Year, National Player of the Year, First Team All-American, and is still the only player in NCAA Division 1 baseball history to win the Triple Crown. He batted .490 with 27 home runs and 95 RBIs. This was after hitting in the .250-.270 range with 5-6 home runs in each of his freshman and sophomore seasons. I asked him once, "What was the difference?" Physically he was the same player but mentally he had made a major adjustment. He explained to me that early in his career when he started a game with a couple hits, he would lose <u>focus </u>and waste at bats because he knew that even if he went hitless the rest of the game he would still end the game with two hits. He also said that if he started 0 for 2 he would press too much knowing that he had to get two hits in his final two at bats to have a good day. Instead, he learned to be totally <u>focused</u> on each at bat no matter the result of his previous at bats. He realized the importance of each at bat. He called this the *Zero for Zero Mentality,* which means that you need to be fully <u>focused</u> during each at bat because each at bat counts just the same in the end. Your goal is to be 1 for 1 each and EVERY at bat!

> *"To create something exceptional, your mindset must be relentlessly focused on the smallest of details." (Unknown)*

Application:

It has been said that winners don't do different things, they just do things differently.

They think differently, they prepare differently, and they handle adversity differently. However, one of the major differences is their ability to focus.

The ability to focus is not only the difference between winning and losing but the difference between average and great.

Average players go through the motions with a "fuzzy" focus that wax and wanes. Some days it's there, other days it's lacking.

Great players, on the other hand, have a clear, on point focus. A focus that is not only precise but consistent and persistent. Winners, whether it be a practice or a game, are so mindful of the task at hand that all potential distractions are null and void.

Famed sports psychologist, the late Dr. Ken Ravizza, explained focus this way- "it simply means being where you need to be when you need to be there". It is about being present and totally invested in the moment.

As the example of Mike Smith illustrates, once he learned how to be where he was supposed to be, when he was supposed to be there, he didn't just go from good to great- he put together one of the finest seasons in college baseball history!

They said it...

"It all started with being hungry up there. You went up to bat with an attitude that you were ready to feast on whatever pitching you'd be facing. Being a hungry hitter meant never being satisfied. That's why I have the record for two hit games, three hit games, four hit games, and five hit games. If I had two hits, I wanted three. If I had three, I wanted four. If I had four, I wanted five. I was always greedy. I always wanted more. I wish I could tell you that out of the sixteen thousand times I batted, I was able to bear down hard every time. No one could do that. But I guarantee I was able to bear down more than anyone else ever did." (Pete Rose)

F.O.C.U.S=FOLLOW ONE COURSE UNTIL SUCCESSFUL

CHAPTER 10

PURPOSEFUL PLANNING & PREPARATION

Purposeful planning and preparation is a detailed proposal for achieving something; the process of being made ready that shows determination and resolve.

> *"You are born to win. But to be a winner you must plan to win, prepare to win, and expect to win."*
> *(Zig Ziglar)*

I feel fortunate to have played for two Hall of Fame coaches during my playing career.

My high school coach, John Tipton, is a member of the Ohio High School Baseball Coaches Hall of Fame. While my college coach, Bob Morgan, had over 1000 career wins and is also a coaching Hall of Famer.

Even though each had their own unique coaching style, both were instrumental in my development as a baseball player.

They differed in their approach on motivation and player development. They each had their own philosophies on how to play winning baseball. One was more offensive minded, while the other stressed pitching and defense.

However, one commonality was that they each had a plan or a system. A plan, that if followed, prepared you to play fundamentally sound, winning baseball.

Both plans, though different, were equally organized, up tempo, and effective when backed with massive action. Both plans stressed the importance of mastering the fundamentals. Each emphasized quality over quantity and the importance of practicing with a game-like focus and tempo.

It has been said that if you fail to plan, you plan to fail.

I can promise you that John Tipton and Bob Morgan coached teams never lost because of lack of planning or preparation. They won way more than they lost and when they did lose it was due to a lack of talent or an unwillingness of their players to carry out their plan.

> *"It's not the will to win that matters, everyone has that, it's the will to prepare to win the matters."*
> *(Paul "Bear" Bryant)*

Application:

In the *Way of the Champions* it is said that the three most important elements of building a champion are preparation, preparation, and preparation.

With that being said, preparation begins with a plan. A plan that is purposefully designed to achieve specific goals that are both measurable and realistic yet challenging.

However, simply having goals with a plan is not enough. In order to achieve your goals, your plan must be backed with massive action. Action that is persistent, consistent, and relentless.

Even then, no matter how meticulous you may be in your planning and preparation, things will not always go as expected and adjustments must be made. The ability and willingness to adjust and adapt in these situations is critical for sustained success.

They said it...

"Goals without commitment are nothing more than wishes. You have to dedicate yourself to your own success and then do whatever it takes day after day. Begin each day by asking, " What can I do today to make it happen?" (Augie Garrido)

IF YOU FAIL TO PLAN, YOU PLAN TO FAIL

CHAPTER 11

POISE

Poise is a calm, self-assured, dignified manner of being, especially during times of stress and adversity; COMPOSURE.

"The key to winning is poise under stress."
(Paul Brown)

In 1992, I was in my junior year at Indiana University and we were down four runs in the seventh as we prepared for our final at bat against the University of Michigan. The fourth hitter due up that inning was our All-American shortstop Mike ("Smitty") Smith. "Smitty" was in the midst of one of the finest seasons in the history of college baseball and is still to this day the only player in Division I baseball history to win the Triple Crown. As the three hitters before him prepared to bat, he told each one of us, "If you guys get on I'll tie this thing up!" After a hit and two base-on- balls, "Smitty" came to the plate with an opportunity to back up his words. After two quick strikes by Michigan's All-Big Ten closer Todd Marion, things were looking bleak. However, after stepping out of the bat-ter's box to regain his <u>composure</u>, he stepped back in the box and launched the next pitch over the left field fence for a grand slam that sent the game into extra innings. Even though we would win the game in the ninth on my game winning RBI single, there is no doubt that the confidence and <u>composure </u>of Mike Smith is the real reason we won the game.

"Every great player has learned the 2 C's: how to concentrate and how to maintain composure."
(Byron Nelson)

Application:

You cannot avoid pressure if you want to achieve greatness. Winners not only don't avoid pressure, they thrive on it. They possess a mental toughness that allows them to remain calm and focused no matter how stressful the situation. This ability is developed via diligent preparation and the confidence created from past successes.

Winners realize that lack of preparation, not competition, is the true root of anxiety. Therefore, they train with an intensity and focus that allows them to quiet their mind, trust their abilities, and compete free of fear, anxiety, and self-doubt.

They said it...

In 1947, Branch Rickey signed Jackie Robinson to a professional contract and on April 14th when he started at first base for the Brooklyn Dodgers, he became the first African American to play in the Major Leagues. But before signing Robinson, Rickey had to make sure that he was willing and able to withstand the racial abuse that he would inevitably face. When Rickey explained to him that he could not react angrily or retaliate against the racial insults, even if they came from his own teammates, Robinson asked, " Are you looking for a negro who is afraid to fight back?" Rickey responded, " I'm looking for a ball player with the guts not to fight back!"

How many of us would have been able to maintain our poise and composure under those conditions?

CONTROL YOUR EMOTIONS, DON'T LET THEM CONTROL YOU

CHAPTER 12

PRIDELESSNESS

Pridelessness is the quality of not having an excessively high opinion of oneself or one's importance; HUMILITY

> *"Humility is not thinking less of yourself.*
> *It's thinking of yourself less."*
> *(Rick Warren)*

The Wheelersburg Pirates were the reigning 2012 Ohio Division III Baseball State Champions but, their chances for a repeat were looking bleak. Even though they'd fought their way to the 2013 championship game, they found themselves down 4-3 in the bottom of the seventh after committing a very uncharacteristic five errors. The Pirates chances looked even bleaker after their lead-off batter popped up to the pitcher. They were now just two outs away from relinquishing their crown to the Bulldogs of Bloom Carroll.

However, an infield single, a fielder's choice, and a RBI single by Dillon Miller tied the score. And just like that, despite their fielding miscues and lackluster performance up to this point, the Pirates now found themselves one run away from becoming back-to-back state champions.

With runners on second and third, the Bulldogs decided to intentionally walk the next hitter to load the bases and put the double play in order. Then after a timely strikeout by Bloom Carroll pitcher Corey Stanley, a double play was no longer needed. The Bulldogs were now just one out away from dodging a bullet and sending the game into extra innings. After two quick strikes on the Pirates Zach Brown, it looked as if extra innings was a very likely possibility.

However, on the 0-2 offering to Brown, the unthinkable happened, as the pitch bounced off catcher Jarrett Peter's mitt and ricocheted to the backstop. Peter's sprinted to the backstop, grabbed the ball with his bare hand, and fired it to Stanley, who was covering the plate but…. it was too late. Cameron Parsley had sprinted from third base and already slid across home plate for the winning run. And just like that the Wheelersburg Pirates were back to back state champions!

Many would say that this was the play of the game. Scoring the winning run in the state championship game, how could it not be?

However, the real play of the game for me occurred minutes after Parsley crossed the plate with the umpires already in the dressing room and the Wheelersburg Pirates repeat title firmly secured.

As Pirate players and coaches sprinted out of the dugout to mob Parsley behind home plate, Wheelersburg head coach, Mike Estep, noticed a dejected Jarrett Peters on all fours face down in the dirt. Despite the pandemonium and excitement of just making history as the head coach of a back to back state champion, Coach Estep did not immediately partake in the celebratory dog pile behind home plate. He did not immediately hug one of his own players or coaches. He did not immediately seek out his wife and daughters in the stands to share in the celebration that was going on all around him. Instead, he walked directly to the dejected Peter's, stooped down beside him, put his arm around his shoulders, and consoled the opposing player who had to feel as if he'd just cost his team, his school, and his community the state championship.

"Don't look down on someone unless you are bending over to help them up." (Unknown)

Mike Estep is a champion. He was a part of three Big Ten Championship teams as an All-Big Ten performer at The Ohio State University. He was now a two time state champion as the Head Coach of Wheelersburg High School. But to me winning baseball games is not what makes Mike Estep a champion. What makes Mike Estep a champion is the <u>humility</u>, class, and character he demonstrated towards Jarrett Peters on a night when he could have very easily joined the rest of his coaches and players in the celebratory dog pile behind home plate.

But instead he saw someone who had fallen down and needed helped up. The celebration could wait.

"Being humble means realizing that we are not on earth to see how important we can become but, to see how much of a difference we can make in the lives of others." (Gordon B. Hinckley)

Application:

Winners play with pride. They take pride in working hard and playing the game the right way. They take pride in being coachable and being a good teammate. But when it comes to their accomplishments and successes they are pride-less. Their humility is what allows them to remain coachable and hungry for continued success; For it is the lack of humility that creates complacency, over confidence, and an unwillingness to continue to learn and grow.

They said it ...

> "I've learned there are two kinds of leaders; those who have been humbled and those who are about to be." (Clint Hurdle)

BE HUMBLE OR BE READY TO BE HUMBLED

CHAPTER 13

PROFESSIONALISM

Professionalism is the conduct and/or qualities that characterize or mark a professional person.

> *"Professional isn't a label you give yourself. It's*
> *a label you hope others will apply to you."*
> *(David Maister)*

For almost thirty years, every high school baseball player in my hometown of Portsmouth, Ohio knew the name Bill Newman. As the head coach of the local American Legion baseball team, he had earned the reputation of not only being a knowledgeable baseball man but, as a tough, no-nonsense disciplinarian. While any player who aspired to play beyond high school was encouraged to play legion baseball, many talented players chose not to due to an unwillingness or fear of not being able to meet his lofty expectations.

I too questioned whether I had what it took to play for such a demanding coach. However, I also knew that if I wanted to play beyond high school, I could not pass on the opportunity to play against better competition and absorb Bill's knowledge of the game. After trying out and making the team, it did not take me long to realize that everything I'd heard about Bill Newman was true. He was tough. He was demanding. He was disciplined. But what I also learned during my time playing for Bill was that he was fair, he was honest, and he was loyal. And even though he had a different way of showing it...he was loving.

Sometimes he told me things I didn't necessarily want to hear, in ways and tones I didn't want to hear them, but I, like a large majority of his former players, loved Bill Newman. Of course his baseball knowledge made us all better baseball players but, more importantly, it was the life lessons that he taught us, through the game of baseball, which made us better men.

Bill Newman passed away several years ago. He is missed by many but his legacy will live on forever. A legacy built not only on baseball but on the professionalism that he exhibited in all aspects of his life.

We live in a society that tends to equate fame, fortune, and titles as the mark of a professional. Bill Newman had none of that. He wasn't famous. He had no fancy initials or titles before or after his name. Nor did he have a lot of money. In fact, he never made a dime coaching baseball, as he volunteered for 29 seasons! But what Bill did have was a clear conscious knowing that he did things the right way. Everything he did, he did with the utmost class, character, honor, dignity, respect, humility, and integrity. And it was because of those things that Bill Newman was THE ultimate professional.

> *"Professionalism is not the job you do;*
> *it's how you do your job."*
> *(Shiv Kiera)*

Application:

A pro baseball player gets paid for their ability to run, hit, throw, catch, and/or field a baseball but professionalism goes well beyond the diamond, a contract, or a paycheck.

Professionalism requires a willingness to do what's right as well as remain humble during times of success. It requires dependability, accountability, and an adherence to solid moral and ethical values both on and of the field.

You see being a pro doesn't mean you are a professional and being a professional doesn't require you to be a pro.

Play the game the right way. Be a good teammate. Be coachable. Be humble. Demonstrate common courtesy and whatever you do, do it with a high level of class, character, and integrity. If you do these things, you are a professional whether you sign a pro contract or not.

They said it...

> "Baseball is about talent, hard work, and strategy. But at the deepest level, it's about love, integrity, and respect." (Pat Gillick)

ACT LIKE YOU'VE BEEN THERE BEFORE

CHAPTER 14

PROGRESSIVE THINKING

Progressive thinking is thinking in a way that is new and innovative.

"If you do what you have always done you
will get what you have always gotten."
(Anthony Robbins)

In 1989, Glenn Hoffman was in the final season of his major league career. After making his major league debut on April 12, 1980 he spent nine seasons as a shortstop for the Boston Red Sox and California Angeles. But as his career was ending his younger brother, Trevor's, was just beginning. After hitting a team leading .371 at the University of Arizona, he was drafted as a shortstop by the Cincinnati Reds in the 11th round of the 1989 Major League Baseball draft.

However, it became evident pretty quickly that the athletic, strong armed shortstop was going to face an uphill battle in his quest to follow in his brothers footsteps. After hitting .212 during his first full season in professional baseball, the Reds organization debated releasing him on multiple occasions. However, Hoffman had one tool that kept him around…his major league quality arm.

"I sat in the dugout game after game watching a young shortstop struggle. He wasn't swinging the bat. But he was athletic and I'd watch him throw across the infield and think about his arm. He had a live arm," said Mike Griffin, former minor league pitching coach for the Cincinnati Reds.

Jim Bowden, the Reds Assistant Director of Player Development at the time, described Hoffman as a "solid fielding shortstop with a gun for an arm but a bat that showed zero promise."

Therefore, at the urging of Griffin and manager Jim Lett, the Reds organization came up with a plan.

With the blessing of Red's farm director "Chief" Bender, Griffin and Lett approached Hoffman with their idea on how they felt he could best extend his professional baseball career and realize his dream of playing in "The Show". However, it wasn't as a short-stop…is was as a pitcher.

"I've learned that most players are hesitant at such a suggestion", recalled Griffin. "But Trevor was all on board. He jumped at the chance."

So in June 1990, Trevor Hoffman took his 95 mile per hour fastball down to the bullpen for the first bullpen session of his professional career.

Three years later, on April 6, 1993, he made his major league debut for the Florida Marlins, who had claimed him in the expansion draft. Twenty years later, on September 29, 2010, he would head to the bullpen one final time as he prepared to make his final major league appearance for the Milwaukee Brewers.

Today, Trevor Hoffman is a member of the Major League Baseball Hall of Fame and second on Major League Baseball's all-time career saves list behind Mariano Rivera.

However, none of that would have been possible without the progressive thinking of the Cincinnati Reds organization and the open mindedness and adaptability of Trevor Hoffman.

"The measure of intelligence is the ability to change."
(Albert Einstein)

Application:

Don't let traditions and stubbornness paralyze your progress to success. Be humble enough to be coachable. Be receptive to new ideas. Be willing to think outside the box and find better ways of doing things. Ask questions and never lose your eagerness to learn and grow.

They said it...

> "Learning never ends. Even failures and losses have value if you are open to learning from them and figuring out what you need to know in order to do better the next time. It's always important to know what you don't know. The real joy in sports and any endeavor is the never ending acquiring of knowledge and experiences and then building

upon them so that you feel like your life is moving peak to peak. Know that there will be valleys in between, but that as long as you keep moving forward, you will climb to the top again." (Augie Garrido)

KNOW WHAT YOU DON'T KNOW

CHAPTER 15

PURSUIT OF EXCELLENCE

The pursuit of excellence is the act or process of going after extreme excellence

"Perfection is not attainable but, if we chase
perfection we can catch excellence."
(Vince Lombardi)

One of the greatest examples on the pursuit of excellence was a story I heard about Joey Votto in 2006 while he was playing for the Chattanooga Lookouts, the AA affiliate of the Cincinnati Reds. I was told that the Lookout's were playing a night game and that Votto's dad was in town to watch his son play. Considering the closeness of their relationship and the fact that Mr. Votto had traveled all the way from Canada to see his son play, I'm sure Joey was looking forward to playing in front of his dad and spending some time together after the game. As we have now become accustomed to, Votto was the best hitter in the park that night. He went 4 for 4 and was named player of the game. However, I was told that one of his hits was a pitch on the outside part of the plate that he should have hit the opposite way. Instead he pulled it and fortunately for him, he was still able to hit it well enough to get a hit. Even though he didn't hit it like he was supposed to, he could have very easily left the park with the rest of his teammates, went out to eat with his dad, and been satisfied with the fact that he'd went 4 for 4 and had been named player of the game. However, he knew that as he advanced up the ranks he was not going to be able to get by with not hitting the ball where it is was pitched. Therefore, instead of leaving the park with the rest of his teammates he grabbed a bucket of baseballs and headed to the batting cage with his dad to specifically work on hitting the outside pitch the opposite way. While the rest of his teammates were long gone, hanging out with their girlfriends, or drinking a beer at the local pub, Joey Votto and his dad were in the batting cage alone working on his swing ...even after a 4 for 4 performance! Votto's season would culminate with him winning the Southern League Most Valuable Player Award and eventually being called up to the major leagues the next season. Since then he has earned the reputation of being one of the best hitters in all of baseball and approaching a career that could be worthy of hall of fame status. However, none of that would be possible without his continuous pursuit of excellence.

> **"Desire is the key to motivation, but its determination and commitment to an unrelenting pursuit of your goal-a commitment to excellence-that will enable you to attain the success you seek."**
> **(Mario Andretti)**

Application:

Success requires hard work, discipline, and a willingness to be uncomfortable. However, once you reach your goals and achieve success, you must be willing to establish new goals that require even harder work, more discipline, and a willingness to be even more uncomfortable.

Average players often become complacent or even intimidated by success. They are unwilling or fearful to raise the bar and challenge themselves to be even better. They are content with the status quo and see their work ethic, level of discipline, and state of discomfort as being good enough.

Great players on the other hand are never satisfied. They realize that success is a never ending journey that will always require harder work, more discipline, and a willingness to be even more uncomfortable than the time before.

They said it ...

"If a ballplayer is satisfied, he's going to slip. You have to keep fighting to improve." (Nellie Fox)

COMPLACENCY IS THE ENEMY OF EXCELLENCE

CHAPTER 16

PERSEVERANCE

Perseverance is the continued effort to do or achieve something despite difficulties, failure, or opposition; STEADFASTNESS

"Winners never quit and quitters never win"
(Vince Lombardi)

When I think of <u>perseverance</u> I think of my former professional teammate James Lofton. At 5'9" 160lb., the fact that he was even drafted by the Cincinnati Reds was a surprise to many. While I thought he was a solid player, I too had my doubts about his ability to play in the major leagues. After hitting a combined .247 in four seasons in Class A ball, the Reds had their doubts as well, and gave him his unconditional release. For many, this would have been the end of their baseball career and the beginning of a career in the real world. However, James wasn't quite ready for the real world and signed on with the independent league Tri-City Posse. If you are not familiar with the world of independent baseball, this is the bottom rung of professional baseball. Independent leagues have no affiliation with Major League Baseball. It essentially means that your baseball career is on life support. After four seasons in the independent leagues and a solid .293 batting average, James was signed by the Boston Red Sox organization. For most, simply getting signed by a major league organization would have been vindication enough but, for James his journey wasn't complete. After hitting .315 in 29 games at Double A, he received a promotion to Boston's Triple A affiliate, the Pawtucket Red Sox, one step from the major leagues. Then after hitting .318 in 42 games at Pawtucket, the diminutive, once released, long shot, James Lofton, was called up to the big leagues to start at shortstop for the Boston Red Sox! <u>When others said no, he said yes. When others said you're too small, he said I'm big enough. When others said quit, he said continue on. And because of his perseverance, he will always be known as James Lofton, the former Big Leaguer!</u>

"Remember that guy that gave up? Neither does anyone else."
(Unknown)

Application:

The path to success is a journey. A journey filled with peaks and valleys. While we all desire to reach the peaks, the valleys are inevitable. If you are truly challenging yourself, it's not a matter of if, but when you will be faced with adversity, setbacks, failures, and/or obstacles potentially impeding your path to success.

But the real question is, how will you respond when you are in the valleys? When things aren't going your way and the deck seems stacked against you.

Will you be a camper or a climber?

When in the valleys, losers tend to camp out, enjoying the warmth of the fire and the comfort of their shelter. Either too scared, too lazy, or not caring enough to make the climb.

But winners on the other hand, load their backpacks, tighten their bootstraps, and climb the mountain. Sure the journey is hard, time consuming, and sometimes filled with adversity, setbacks, failures, and/or obstacles attempting to deter and discourage them from reaching their goal(s); however, nothing is going to keep them from reaching the mountain top. No matter what they face, they don't make excuses or give up but, instead they simply continue to climb and find a way to persevere.

They said it...

> "It's hard to beat a person that never gives up."
> (Babe Ruth)

STAY THE COURSE

CHAPTER 17

PERSPECTIVE

Perspective is the capacity to view things in their true relations or relative importance.

"Perspective is the way we see things when we look at them from a certain distance and it allows us to appreciate their true value."
(Rafael Pino)

I wish more people had the opportunity to spend time in the baseball locker room. For it is there that I got a perspective on the world that very few get to experience.

The baseball locker room is a melting pot; a melting pot that allowed me to play with a diversity of race, creed, and nationalities.

I played with players from Canada, Venezuela, Puerto Rico, the Dominican Republic, and every corner of the United States. And while we were all different, we were all the same.

Sure we all looked different, spoke different, and had different views on the world. Views that were shaped by our families, geographical upbringings, and individual life experiences; but at our core, we all valued the same love, respect, and need for acceptance.

It is because of those things that we loved each other, respected each other, and accepted each other despite our differences.

And it is because of those things that we developed a camaraderie and brotherhood that can never be broken.

While baseball gave me a perspective on life, it took death to give me a perspective on baseball.

Less than two years after I played my last game I lost my grand-mother and I can promise you that the pain inflicted by the "death" of a baseball career paled in comparison to the pain and heartache caused by the loss of a loved one.

For the longest time baseball was my love and passion. Therefore, when my career fell short there was a void left in my heart that could never be filled…so I thought.

However, the death of my grandmother made me realize that baseball is not what life is all about. Life is about people and while I miss playing the game of baseball, I miss the people I played it with more than I miss the game itself.

Sure I miss the competition and the process of preparation. However, my competitive spirit and will to prepare has never left me. In my role as a husband, father, and nurse practitioner, it has simply been channeled in a different and more important direction.

"Baseball is just a walk of life. Everything you do in this game you do in life. And everything you do in life you do in this game." (Cal Ripken Sr.)

Application:

Maintaining a proper perspective is crucial for success in the game of baseball.

It's important not because it helps you throw harder, hit further, or run faster but because it creates a calmness that allows you to control your emotions, think more clearly, and keep things in their proper level of significance.

We often refer to the game as a "war" or a "battle" and treat the outcome as if our life depends on it. But in reality neither are true.

As a fighter pilot in World War II and the Korean War, Ted Williams fought in many battles but, none were on the baseball field.

Lou Gehrig announcing to the world that he had a terminal illness that would eventually bear his name was true life and death.

I know that referring to a game as a "war" or a "battle" is only a figure of speech but, always remember that baseball is nothing more than a game.

A game that has tremendous value because of the lessons, relationships, and memories it creates.

But the game and its outcomes are not nearly as important as we sometimes make them out to be.

They said it...

"Baseball is a lot like life. It's day-to-day existence, full of ups and downs. You make most of your opportunities in baseball as you do in life." (Ernie Harwell)

"In baseball, democracy shines its clearest. The only race that matters is the race to the bag. The creed is the rule book. And color, merely something to distinguish one team's uniform from another's." (Ernie Harwell)

KEEP THINGS IN PERSPECTIVE

CONCLUSION

When I reflect on my time playing the game of baseball I often think of the beginning and the end.

In the beginning I was just a young boy with no clue of the journey that lay ahead. I threw a ball against the wall for hours at a time, often well after dark under the spotlight of the corner streetlight post.

All the while dreading to hear my dad or mom call my name, letting me know that it was time to come inside.I played sandlot games in the backyard almost daily, often times to the equivalent of a quadruple-header.

At the time I had no concept of purpose, passion, positive mindset, perspiration equity, pursuit of excellence, poise, or perseverance. I had no idea that there were only 750 Major League Baseball players in the entire world!I had no idea that only 0.5% of high school seniors get drafted into professional baseball. I had no idea that only 10% of those drafted every make the major leagues.

I had never heard baseball referred to as a game of failure because even the best hitters in the game make an out 70% of the time.I had no concept of any of that. All I knew was that I loved playing the game of baseball and that the practices were too short and the time between games was too long.

I wanted to be a Major League Baseball Player like my hometown hero's Al Oliver, Don Gullett, Gene Tenace, Larry Hisle, and Pat Borders. And the summer evenings spent listening to Joe Nuxhull and Marty Brenneman on the radio made me dream specifically of playing for the The Big Red Machine like my favorite player Pete Rose.

In 1992, I came one step closer to realizing that dream when I was drafted by the Cincinnati Reds. As you can imagine, the thrill of getting drafted by my home state team, the team I'd cheered for since I was a child, was euphoric. But the euphoria was short lived. Only weeks into my professional baseball career, I slid headfirst into second base, a la Pete Rose. I'd performed this same slide hundreds of times but this time something was different. My right wrist hurt and progressively worsened over the next several weeks to the point that I eventually needed multiple surgeries to repair a fracture. A fracture that essentially ended my career. Just like that it was over.

By this point I was fully aware of purpose, passion, positive mindset, perspiration equity, pursuit of excellence, poise, and perseverance. But all that was drowned out by my sorrow and bitterness towards the game. Why me? What now? These are the questions I asked myself daily. I went back to college and began working towards finishing my degree without any real direction. The only thing I ever wanted in life was no longer an option. My first love had dumped me.

But after a few years of self-pity I had an epiphany. Instead of using baseball I was letting baseball use me. You see, in between the beginning and the end was a middle. A middle that spanned 15 years. 15 years that allowed me to travel the United States and Canada playing the game of baseball. A middle that allowed me to play with and against people from all over the world. A middle that had provided me with so many valuable lessons. Lessons that had fully equipped me to be successful in whatever I chose to do – IF I applied them.

Eventually the sorrow went away, the bitterness lessened, and the clarity of my future came into focus.

I regained my positive mindset. I eventually found my new purpose and tackled it with passion. I developed a plan for success by establishing new goals and backing it with massive action. I became fully committed and surrounded myself with positive influencers and mentors. And just like in baseball I experienced "failure" and had challenges and obstacles I had to overcome. But with poise, perseverance, and a continuous pursuit of excellence I was able to overcome them. You see what I found is that even though the "game" had changed, the recipe for success remained the same.

Sure I never achieved my goal of becoming a major leaguer and by some people's standards my baseball career was a failure. For the longest time I felt the same way. But how can my career be a failure if it served as the foundation of some of my most cherished relationships? How can it be a failure if it provided me with so many special memories? How can my career be a failure if it taught me so many valuable lessons that are applicable to everyday life? For it is because of these things – the relationships, memories, and lessons

–that even though I am no longer a part of baseball, baseball will always be a part of me. And it is for that reason that success will always be within my grasp.

"BIG 33" 33 LIFE LESSONS LEARNED ON THE DIAMOND

Don't be critical of the critics.

Following my freshman season at Indiana University, my hometown newspaper had an article about me titled, "Ramey Struggles". I'm not going to lie, it upset me. I felt embarrassed and betrayed. I had not seen and still have not seen my local newspaper speak of a local high school or college athlete in such a negative way. However, instead of responding verbally or outwardly to the negativity, I used it as motivation and vowed to never give them an opportunity to print a similar article about me in the future. One year later, they ran an article on me being named All-Big Ten. A year after that, I made the front page for being drafted by the Cincinnati Reds. There are two things I have learned about critics. #1 They are always going to be there. #2 They can either be destructive or constructive. The choice is yours!

"The galleries are full of critics. They play no ball, they fight no fights. They make no mistakes because they attempt nothing. Down in the arena are the doers. They make mistakes because they try many things. The man who makes no mistakes lacks boldness and the spirit of adventure. He is the one who never tries anything. His is the brake on the wheel of progress. And yet it cannot be truly said he makes no mistakes, because his biggest mistake is the very fact that he tries nothing, does nothing, except criticize those who do things." (General David M. Shoupe)

Timing is everything.

During the summer of 1990, I was selected to participate in one of the more prestigious collegiate baseball summer leagues. I was signed as a middle infielder. However, two weeks into the season, not one but both of our catchers went down with season ending injuries. With the season well under way, our coaches were scrambling to find a replacement. I had caught sparingly in high school summer ball but, despite my minimal experience, I volunteered to fill in until they found a replacement. Six weeks later I finished the season not only as the starting catcher but, with a pocket full of business cards from professional scouts promising to come watch me play in the fall. The following spring, I was drafted <u>as a catcher</u> by the Cincinnati Reds!

It only takes one.

In an effort to improve my chances of playing college baseball, I wrote letters to several college baseball coaches encouraging them to come watch me play. During the spring of my senior season, two coaches to whom I had written letters, showed up at my game. After a hitless performance and no chances in the field, they left early without saying a word. The very next day, a former assistant coach at Indiana University was at our game. This time, after collecting two hits against a quality pitcher and making several nice plays in the field, he told me after the game that he was going to recommend me for a scholarship. Two weeks later, I signed my national letter of intent to play college baseball at Indiana University. What a difference a day made. Always remember that it only takes one coach on that one day to see that one outstanding performance to make that one recommendation or scholarship offer!

Don't be a but.

It has been said that there is nothing worse than wasted talent. My home town like most towns is full of unfulfilled potential. How many times have we heard that he/she could have done that but... The word but has to constantly torment the mind and pierce the heart of the quitter and the underachiever. Don't be a but!

Don't be a butt.

While we cannot all be great players, we can all be great teammates. Being a great teammate means being humble, unselfish, and making others feel valued. These are the qualities, not statistics or wins and losses, that your teammates will remember. They'll remember you for how you made them feel more than how great of a player you were. Don't be a butt!

Do's and Don'ts

Do…be on time, give good effort, be energetic, have a positive attitude, be passionate, use good body language, be coachable, do more than is required, and be prepared

Don't…try to please everyone, fear change, live in the past, put yourself down, overthink, or ever give up

Be where your feet are.

The good moments in life will come and go quickly. Therefore, we should enjoy them all. One of my biggest regrets as a baseball player is that I never truly enjoyed the moment. I was always looking ahead to the next moment or the next challenge but, by doing that I never got to truly enjoy the moment that I was in. Be mindful of the moment you're in. Enjoy it and cherish it. Make sure you make a conscious effort to enjoy where your feet are.

Don't take it personal.

During my freshman season at Indiana University, I earned the nod as the starting shortstop.Through the first ten games I was struggling at the plate but errorless in the field. My first error came in game #11 against Kansas State. Realizing that errors are part of the game, I shrugged it off and jogged back to the dugout when the inning was over. However, my coach, Bob Morgan, who was known for his militaristic coaching style, wasn't shrugging it off as easily as I was. He proceeded to pull me by my jersey into the clubhouse and tell me that "I wasn't worth a cold can of piss and that I may as well transfer now because I'll never play here". Despite the initial shock, I couldn't help but think back to what my dad had told me years prior, " when a coach stops being critical that means they've stopped caring about you". It wasn't until that moment that I realized how much Coach Morgan truly loved me. Even if he had a different way of showing it.

Control what you can control.

In college, I worried about the recruiting classes behind me. As a pro, I worried about the performances of the other catchers in the organization. But what I eventually realized was that who they recruited or the performance of others was beyond my control. The only things I could truly control were my preparation, effort, and attitude. Make sure you are focusing on the controllables because worrying about the uncontrollables is a waste of your precious time and energy.

If it doesn't challenge you it doesn't change you.

My freshman season at Indiana University was challenging to say the least. Not only was I away from home for the first time but, I was also trying to balance school, baseball, and my social life. And if all that wasn't challenging enough, I was playing for one of the most demanding coaches in all of college baseball. It was uncomfortable. It was a physical and mental grind. At times I wanted to quit. But because I stuck it out it changed me for the better. Not only did it make me better as a baseball player but, it made me a better man.

Failure isn't fatal.

No one likes to fail but I am so thankful for the times that I did. For it is those times that had the most influence on my career and my life. I cried when I got cut. I cried when I was left off my high school baseball teams post season roster. I thought about quitting or transferring when I was struggling early in my college career. But because I persevered through those times I know how to handle failure today. I realize that failure isn't fatal but simply an opportunity to grow, learn, and prove how badly you want something.

If those around you won't change, change those around you.

You can't choose your family; most of the time you can't choose your teammates. But what you can choose is your friends and the teammates you allow to influence you. Choose them wisely. Surround yourself with those who motivate and inspire you in a positive way. If you are surrounding yourself with "friends" and teammates who aren't doing those things you need to change them before they change you. Your future success and more importantly your life depend on it.

Don't Feed the Stray Cats

Most of us at one time or another have opened our front door and found a stray cat lurking on our porch. It purrs and rubs against our leg trying to entice us to feed it. It is at that moment that we must make a decision- feed it or shoo it away. If you feed it you may own a pet. If you shoo it away it will wander next-door and try to entice your neighbor. As a baseball player you will have stray cats wander onto your porch except the porch is your mind and the stray cats come in the form of fear, anxiety, and self-doubt. If you shoo them away they will move on to the next "porch" but if you feed them they will turn into a roaring lion that will devour your path to success!

Bond Like the Sequoia's

I heard my former teammate and current Western Michigan Head baseball Coach Bill Gernon speak once on the importance of togetherness and team chemistry. In his speech he used the sequoia tree as an illustration. He explained that the sequoia tree is the world's largest living organism but, despite its enormous size it has a very shallow root system. However, below the surface, the roots of the Sequoia bond together so tightly that the trees are able to not only stand upright but survive the high winds of a hurricane. Make sure your team is bonding like the sequoias for it is team chemistry, camaraderie, and togetherness, not talent, that will allow you to weather the storms.

Have an Attitude of Gratitude.

In 1993, I played with an 18-year-old Venezuelan shortstop named Johnny Carvajal. I was in awe that a player so young could possess the arm strength, body control, and near flawless hands at such a young age. I wondered to myself how could a kid so young, be so good? I then found out that his first "glove" was half of a milk jug taped to his hand. This not only helped me understand how he was so good at a young age but it also made me feel guilty for being upset when my dad did not get me the $300 Rawling's glove that

I wanted for Christmas. Be thankful for what you have instead of focusing on what you don't have.

Be willing to drink from the water hose.

In 2014, the late Tony Robichaux, former head baseball coach at Louisiana Lafayette, had this to say about the type of players he likes to recruit, "I want players who are willing to drink out of the water hose, not the guy whose mom he is bringing him a Powerade in the third inning". He was essentially saying that he wanted players with grit, guts, and mental toughness. Make sure you are willing to drink from the water hose.

> "Gold medals aren't really made of gold. They're made of sweat, determination, and a hard-to-find alloy called guts." (Dan Gable)

People matter most.

During my senior season of high school, we entered the post season ranked #4 in the state. We had a solid team with aspirations of winning a state championship. However, in the district finals we lost a 3-2 heartbreaker to Lancaster (Ohio) High School, the #1 ranked team in the state. After shaking the victor's hands, I remember sitting on the top step of the dugout, staring straight ahead, replaying the game in my mind. Then I caught a glimpse of Lance Daniels untying his cleats and preparing to put them in his bag. At that moment I began to cry uncontrollably. For it was at that moment that I realized that the loss was a heartbreaker not because we lost the game but because I was never going to play with my teammates and childhood friends ever again.

It's not how good you are on your best day but how good you are on your worst day that matters.

During my time as a catcher in the Cincinnati Reds organization, Joe Oliver was the starting major league catcher. If Joe Oliver and I each made our best throws to second base you could not tell much difference in the two. However, the real difference was the fact that Joe Oliver made his best throw more consistent than I made mine. This consistency of excellence is often the difference between great and good. A lot of players are great on their best day but, the best players are great even on their worst day.

If you're on time you're late.

Jack was the team's starting catcher so when I showed up for the game and saw another player behind the plate I assumed he was injured. However, I quickly found out that Jack wasn't hurt at all but had been sat out for showing up late for pregame batting practice. As a former player, realizing how special each and every opportunity you have to play the game truly is, I thought how sad that Jack missed out on one of his finite opportunities because he simply couldn't be on time. Don't be like Jack! Show up early so that you don't chance missing out on one of your precious opportunities to play the game.

You earn your spotlight.

My former American Legion baseball coach, Bill Newman, was an old school, no nonsense baseball coach. He was a coach that expected the routine plays be made and the fundamentals be

76

mastered. He wasn't going to give you praise for simply doing what you were supposed to do. However, when you did do something exceptional he would stand on the top step of the dugout and yell loud enough for everyone in the stadium to hear, "Hot Tamale!" If you were fortunate enough to be the player who got the "Hot Tamale!"it made you feel like there was a magical spotlight beaming down on top of you. You could literally feel your chest fill with pride because you knew that Coach Newman didn't give them out freely. You see we all enjoy the spotlight once and awhile but what we fail to realize is that the spotlight <u>must</u> be earned. And when Bill Newman yelled "Hot Tamale!"and put the spotlight on you, you knew that you had truly earned it.

Stay the course.

In the fall of 1992, I showed up at Indiana University as one of six recruited shortstops on the roster. While we all had impressive high school resumes, we also realized that only one us could start. It still amazes me to this day that I gained the starting nod by simply staying the course. You see after one failed out, one partied his way out of the game, and two got homesick and transferred, the competition between six was quickly down to two. I eventually won the starting nod not because I was more talented but because I simply showed up everyday, went to class, fought through the homesickness, and didn't belly up to the bar every night. Stay the course and good things will eventually happen.

Attitude matters.

Let each letter of the alphabet have a value equal to it's sequence in the alphabetical order:

A	B	C	D	E	F	G	H	I	J	K	L	M	N	O	P	Q	R	S	T	U	V	W	X	Y	Z
1	2	3	4	5	6	7	8	9	10	11	12	13	14	15	16	17	18	19	20	21	22	23	24	25	26

A	B	I	L	I	T	Y			
1	3	9	12	9	20	25		=	**79**

S	K	I	L	L	S		
19	11	9	12	12	19	=	**82**

K	N	O	W	L	E	D	G	E		
11	14	15	23	12	5	4	7	5	=	**96**

H	A	R	D		W	O	R	K		
8	1	18	4		23	15	18	11	=	**98**

A	T	T	I	T	U	D	E		
1	20	20	9	20	21	4	5	=	**100**

Just a coincidence or not? I don't think so

The best ability is availability.

The best ability of any athlete is availability. The ability to run fast, throw hard, or hit far is useless if you aren't available to play. Unfortunately injuries happen, they are a part of the game. But make sure you are doing your part in keeping yourself healthy. Get your rest, eat right, and do your preventative maintenance. Pre-habilitation is always easier than rehabilitation.

Don't kill the grass.

My high school baseball coach, John Tipton, had a 9 to 5 rule. This meant that after each half inning we had to get 9 men off the field before they got 5 on and 5 men on the field before they got 9 off. This was a rule put into place to force us to hustle on and off the field. If he ever thought someone was going a little to slow for his liking or standing in one spot a little too long he'd yell, "Quit killing the grass!" Make sure your coach doesn't ever accuse you of killing the grass.

Optional isn't optional.

Every now and then a coach will have an "optional" practice. Most view this as it's optional whether I want to show up or not but what it really means is that it's optional whether you want to show your coach how badly you want to play. Show up and make sure you always pass the "optional" test.

Just because you're small doesn't mean you can't do big things.

My best friend's son, Alex, plays travel baseball. He is eight years old playing for a team of much older players. Because of the age difference he is not only much younger but also much smaller. One game after pitching 4 scoreless innings his dad, Pat, heard him say to himself " just because I'm small doesn't mean I can't do big things." When Pat asked Alex where he'd heard that from Alex replied, "nowhere, that's just what I tell myself in my head." As a 5'2" 105 pound freshman, I wish I would have had the same wisdom and mindset as 8 year old Alex Rigsby.

Fight the elements.

At least once every fall, with the rain pouring down, we'd head to the clubhouse expecting a sign on the board announcing that practice was cancelled. However, despite the poor weather conditions, practice would be on as planned. Within minutes of being on the field our uniforms would be saturated, our cleats would be packed with mud, and our finger tips would be slippery. If that wasn't bad enough the water logged balls felt like shot puts. None the less, Coach Morgan would continue to pound us ground ball after ground ball as if it was hot, sunny, and dry. If we missed a ball or made a bad throw he'd yell, "You gotta fight the elements!" Sometimes playing conditions aren't going to be ideal but excuses aren't going to help anything. All you can do is grip the ball a little tighter, focus a little harder, and do whatever you have to do to conquer the elements.

Blessed to be stressed.

Playing college and professional baseball was challenging. It was hard work. It was time consuming. It required great sacrifice and commitment. Sometimes it was down right stressful. But now that I can reflect on all the relationships, life lessons, and memories I've created because of baseball, I know without hesitation that I'd do it all again. I didn't realize it while I was playing but I was truly blessed to be stressed.

Make your bed.

Another good read is <u>Make Your Bed</u> by Admiral William H. McRaven. In the book he explains why the military is so particular about how you make your bed:

> "*Every morning in basic SEAL training, my instructors, who at the time were all Vietnam veterans, would show up in my barracks room and the first thing they would inspect was your bed. If you did it right, the corners would be square, the covers pulled tight, the pillow centered just under the headboard and the extra blanket folded neatly at the foot of the rack — that's Navy talk for bed.*

It was a simple task — mundane at best. But every morning we were required to make our bed to perfection. It seemed a little ridiculous at the time, particularly in light of the fact that were aspiring to be real warriors, tough battle-hardened SEALs, but the wisdom of this simple act has been proven to me many times over.

If you make your bed every morning you will have accomplished the first task of the day. It will give you a small sense of pride, and it will encourage you to do another task and another and another. By the end of the day, that one task completed will have turned into many tasks completed. Making your bed will also reinforce the fact that little things in life matter. If you can't do the little things right, you will never do the big things right."

Make sure you are making <u>your</u> bed. You can't accomplish the big things without first mastering the little things.

Work while you wait.

It's hard sitting the bench. It's hard being a backup. It's easy to think you'll never get your chance. It's easy to think you are practicing for nothing. But in order to be ready when your name is called you must continue to work, while you wait for your opportunity. Even though you aren't the #1 you have to prepare like the #1 so you can perform like a #1 and stay the #1. The only way you can do this is to continue to <u>work while you wait</u>.

Why not me?

When I suffered my wrist injury that essentially ended my career, I frequently asked myself, "Why me?" But what I've learned is if you are gonna ask "why me" for every negative in your life you need to also ask "why me" for every positive in your life. The real question I should have asked was, "Why not me?".

Play each game likes it's your last.

One of my favorite books is <u>The Last Lecture.</u> The book was written by Randy Pausch shortly after he'd been diagnosed with terminal pancreatic cancer. One thing he says in the book is that "time is the most valuable thing we have, use it wisely because one day you may realize that you have less than you thought you had". Two weeks after my manager and former big league catcher Donnie Scott called me into his office to tell me that he felt I had the potential to catch in the Big Leagues, I injured my wrist sliding head first into second base. I had no clue at the time that my career was essentially over, not realizing that I had less time to play the game than I thought I had. Play each game like it's your last because it just might be.

We are all day-to-day!

Baseball is not life.

"*Baseball is Life*" this is the slogan commonly seen on t-shirts, sweatshirts, and other baseball paraphernalia. As a player, I truly felt baseball was my life. It was my passion. It was my identity. But what I've come to realize is that until you experience death you can not truly understand the meaning of life. Since my baseball career has been over I have lost both grandparents, aunts, uncles, friends, former coaches and teammates, and three former players. As a nurse practitioner, I see death on a regular basis. These experiences have made me understand that baseball is <u>not</u> life but only a part of life. I have learned that the "death" of a baseball career hurts a whole lot less than the death of a loved one.

Just weeks in to my career as a nurse practitioner, I sat in my office searching for the right words to say. A patient in his early 50's had come to see me the week prior complaining of a chronic cough. After trying a course of antibiotics and seeing no improvement in his symptoms, I decided to order a chest X-ray. Then, when the chest X-ray came back abnormal, I ordered a CAT scan of his chest to further evaluate the abnormality. The results of the CAT scan showed he had lung cancer. And not just lung cancer but, small cell lung cancer, the most aggressive type. With his son and wife waiting by his side, I prayed for the right words to say as I got ready to inform them that their father and husband would probably die in less than a year. If there was ever a situation that I needed poise, this was it. If there was ever a moment that I needed to demonstrate powerful leadership, this was the moment. And if there was ever a time that I needed to encourage a positive mindset and perseverance, this was the time. I can't remember the exact words I said that day but, I do remember leaving the room thinking that I had handled myself well. I got some confirmation of this several months later when the family sent me a card thanking me for my compassion and care. Since that time I've had many similar conversations. This is the reality of my life today. I no longer prepare to hit 95 mile per hour fastballs but, instead I have to be prepared to make decisions on a daily basis that impact people's health and potentially their lives. The "game" I'm playing today is much more important. But what I have found is that the recipe for winning in sports is the same for winning in life. And for this reason, even though my baseball career has long been over, my will to prepare to win has carried on. While there may be some that questioned my ability as a baseball player, I hope that no one questioned my will to prepare. It was because of my will to prepare and the will of my teammates, that I was able to be a part of many winning teams. And with the winning came many awards but, the greatest award, is that by preparing to win in the game of baseball, baseball prepared me to win in the game of life.

The P's To Winning

POTENTIAL: The latent qualities or abilities that may be developed and lead to future success

> "Potential means you haven't done anything yet." (Bill Parcells)

PHYSICAL TALENT: An athlete's innate ability that enhances one's potential for success

> "Hard work beats talent when talent doesn't work hard." (Tim Notke)

PURPOSE: A person's intentions, objectives, and sense of resolve or determination

> "The two most important days of your life are the day you're born and the day you find out why." (Mark Twain)

PASSION: An intense desire or enthusiasm for something

"Nothing great is achieved without enthusiasm." (Ralph Waldo Emerson)

POSITIVE MINDSET: An established set of values or beliefs marked by optimism

"Whether you think you can or think you can't you are right." (Henry Ford)

PERSPIRATION EQUITY: An increased value in something earned from labor or hard work

"No one ever drowned in sweat." (Lou Holtz)

PERSONAL SACRIFICE: Giving up something you want or desire for the greater good or to help others

"No man achieves great success who is unwilling to make great sacrifice." (Napoleon Hill)

POWERFUL LEADERSHIP: The act of leading with great power, prestige, and influence

"A leader is one who knows the way, goes the way, and shows the way." (John Maxwell)

POSITIVE PERIPHERY: The perimeter of a circle that has a good, affirmative, or constructive quality or attribute

"You are the average of the five people you spend the most time with." (Jim Rohn)

PRECISE, PERSISTENT FOCUS: A prolonged, enduring concentration level that is marked by consistency, exactness, accuracy, and attention to detail

> "The successful warrior is an average man with a laser-like focus." (Bruce Lee)

PURPOSEFUL PLANNING & PREPARATION: A detailed proposal for achieving something; the process of being made ready that shows determination & resolve

> "Failing to plan is planning to fail." (Alan Lakein)

> "It's not the will to win that matters, everyone has that, it's the will to prepare to win that matters." (Paul Bryant)

POISE: A calm self-assured dignified manner of being especially during times of stress and adversity

> "The key to winning is poise under stress." (Paul Brown)

PRIDELESSNESS: The quality of not having an excessively high opinion of oneself or one's importance; HUMILITY

> "Humility is not thinking less of yourself, but thinking of yourself less." (C.S. Lewis)

PROFESSIONALISM: The conduct or qualities that characterize or mark a professional person

> "Professionalism is not the job you do, it's how you do your job." (Shiv Khera)

PROGRESSIVE THINKING: Thinking in a way that is new and innovative

> "If you do what you have always done you will get what you have always gotten." (Anthony Robbins)

PURSUIT OF EXCELLENCE: The act or process of going after extreme excellence

> "Excellence is doing ordinary things extraordinarily well." (John William Gardner)

PERSEVERANCE: A steadfastness in doing something despite difficulty or delay in achieving success

> "A quitter never wins and a winner never quits." (Napoleon Hill)

PERSPECTIVE: Perspective is the capacity to view things in their true relations or relative importance.

> "Perspective is the way we see things when we look at them from a certain distance and it allows us to appreciate their true value." (Rafael Pino)

The Diamond of Success

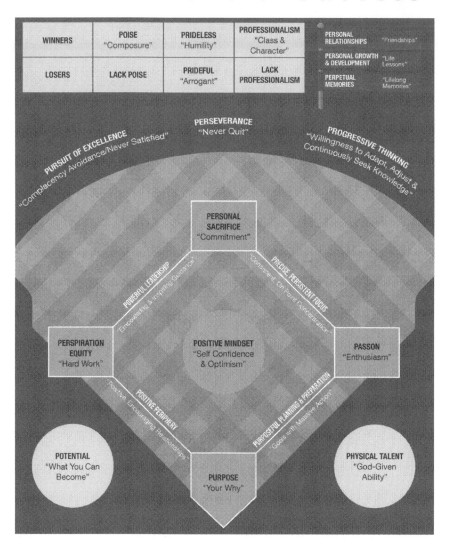

WINNERS	POISE "Composure"	PRIDELESS "Humility"	PROFESSIONALISM "Class & Character"
LOSERS	LACK POISE	PRIDEFUL "Arrogant"	LACK PROFESSIONALISM

PERSONAL RELATIONSHIPS	"Friendships"
PERSONAL GROWTH & DEVELOPMENT	"Life Lessons"
PERPETUAL MEMORIES	"Lifelong Memories"

PERSEVERANCE "Never Quit"

PURSUIT OF EXCELLENCE "Complacency Avoidance/Never Satisfied"

PROGRESSIVE THINKING "Willingness to Adapt, Adjust & Continuously Seek Knowledge"

PERSONAL SACRIFICE "Commitment"

POWERFUL LEADERSHIP "Empowering & Inspiring Guidance"

PRECISE, PERSISTENT FOCUS "Consistent, On Point Concentration"

PERSPIRATION EQUITY "Hard Work"

POSITIVE MINDSET "Self Confidence & Optimism"

PASSON "Enthusiasm"

POSITIVE PERIPHERY "Positive, Encouraging Relationships"

PURPOSEFUL PLANNING & PREPARATION "Goals with Massive Action"

POTENTIAL "What You Can Become"

PURPOSE "Your Why"

PHYSICAL TALENT "God-Given Ability"

CREDITS

Bastian, Jordan. *Selfless Halladay Defined by Tireless Work Ethic.* *https://www.mlb.com/news/roy-halladay-led-by-example-with-work-ethic-c260892610*

Center, Bill. *Hoffman's Early Transformation from SS to P.* *https://www.mlb.com/news/how-trevor-hoffman-transformed-into-a-pitcher-c281075154*

Garrido, Augie. Life is Yours to Win: Lessons Forged from the Purpose, Passion, and Magic of Baseball.

Hamilton, Josh. Beyond Belief: Finding the Strength to Come Back.

Lewis, Michael. Moneyball: The Art of Winning An Unfair Game.

Lynch, Jerry & Huang, Chungliang Al. The Way of the Champion: Lessons from Sun Tzu's The Art of War and Other Tao Wisdom for Sport & Life.

Mainieri, Demie. The Mainieri Factor: Promoting Baseball With a Passion from Miami Dade to NotreDame, LSU, and the Chicago Cubs.

Rose, Pete. <u>Play Hungry: The Making of a Baseball Player.</u>

Thompson, Frank. *Thank You, Coach Michael Estep, For Molding Fine Young Men.* <u>*Allthingswildlyconsidered.blogspot.com*</u>

Made in the USA
Monee, IL
29 January 2020